Pillars of Accountability
A Risk Management Guide for Nonprofit Boards
2nd Edition

by Melanie L. Herman

Copyright © 2006
by the Nonprofit Risk Management Center

ISBN 1-893210-22-7

**Nonprofit
Risk Management
Center**

About the Nonprofit Risk Management Center

The Nonprofit Risk Management Center is dedicated to helping community-serving nonprofits prevent harm, conserve resources, preserve assets, and free up resources for mission-critical activities. The Center provides technical assistance on risk management, liability, and insurance matters; publishes easy-to-use written materials; designs and delivers workshops and conferences; and offers competitively priced consulting services. The Center is an independent nonprofit organization that doesn't sell insurance or endorse specific insurance providers. For more information on the products and services available from the Center, call (202) 785-3891 or visit our Web sites at **www.nonprofitrisk.org**, **www.NonprofitCARES.org**, **www.MyRiskManagementPlan.org**, and **www.riskmanagementclassroom.org**.

Nonprofit Risk Management Center
1130 Seventeenth Street, NW - Suite 210
Washington, DC 20036
(202) 785-3891 / Fax: (202) 296-0349
www.nonprofitrisk.org

Staff

Sheryl Augustine, *Customer Service Representative*
Melanie L. Herman, *Executive Director*
Barbara B. Oliver, *Director of Communications*
John C. Patterson, *Senior Program Director*
George L. Head, Ph.D., *Special Advisor*

Acknowledgments

The Nonprofit Risk Management Center is grateful for the support of the Public Entity Risk Institute (PERI), which provided a generous grant to support the cost of publishing the first edition of this book. For more information about PERI, visit the organization's Web site at **www.riskinstitute.org**.

The author expresses thanks to Tim Delaney for his thought-provoking Foreword and gratitude to the following persons who offered helpful suggestions concerning the second edition of this book: Jennifer Chandler Hauge of Independent Sector; Kate Dewey of McCrory & McDowell; Kim St. Bernard of Girl Scouts of the USA; Ann Shanklin of NIAC; and Jo Sachiko Uehara. Chapter 3, Fiscal Integrity, was based on the Fiscal Integrity Module of Pillars of Accountability, developed by Jeanne Peters of CompassPoint (www.compasspoint.org). Chapter 4, Leadership Sustainability, was based on the Leadership Sustainability Module of Pillars of Accountability, developed by Don Tebbe with Tom Adams, both of TransitionGuides. The chapter introduction was based, in part, on work by Karen Gaskins Jones of JLH Associates, a TransitionGuides Senior Associate.

Table of Contents

Foreword

by Tim Delaney, Esq.*

Beware Buzzwords

W*ebster's Dictionary* defines a buzzword as "an important-sounding, usually technical word or phrase often of little meaning used chiefly to impress laymen." Wikipedia elaborates: "Buzzwords appear ubiquitously but their actual meanings often remain unclear. Buzzwords ... have the function of impressing or obscuring meaning." And WordNet offers the following meaning: "stock phrases that have become nonsense through endless repetition."

The words "accountability" and "transparency" have not been reduced to complete nonsense, but there can be no dispute that the terms have become ubiquitous recently as accountants, lawyers, and other consultants have been invoking the terms endlessly, repeating these important-sounding words to impress various audiences. Those audiences, in turn, have been tossing the words around haphazardly—to the point that the real meanings of "accountability" and "transparency" seem unclear to speakers and listeners alike. Speakers say the terms and listeners politely nod, but no one really knows what is meant. When that happens, it's time to take a step back to gain some perspective.

*Tim Delaney is the Founder and President of the Center for Leadership, Ethics and Public Service based in Phoenix, AZ.

"Accountability" Has Become a Buzzword

Intrigued at how people today appear to be using the term "accountability" as shorthand for different things, and inspired by Joseph Rost, who found 221 definitions of another popular word—"leadership"—when writing *Leadership for the Twenty-First Century* (1990), I set out to review what "accountability" means today.

First, I turned to dictionaries, where I found dozens of different definitions of "accountability." *Random House* defines it to mean "the state of being accountable, liable, or answerable." WordNet offers this twist, "responsibility to someone or for some activity," while Centipedia.com notes it means "the aspects of responsibility involving giving a statistical or judicial explanation for events." Even the *Department of Defense Dictionary of Military and Associated Words* has a view: "The obligation ... for keeping accurate records of property, documents, or funds. The person having this obligation may or may not have actual possession of the property, documents, or funds. Accountability is concerned primarily with records, while responsibility is concerned primarily with custody, care, and safekeeping."

Thinking that dictionaries might be offering different distinctions to meet market niches, I then turned to the Internet to see if there is a universally-accepted usage in the real world. That search confirmed that the word "accountability" is extremely popular, with more than 225 million hits on Google (and a seemingly equal number of interpretations). That search also revealed the term is perceived to be extremely marketable, in that more than 290 books have the word "accountability" in their titles—books about corporate, education, governmental, leadership, military, nonprofit, personal, and other aspects of accountability. Wikipedia's on-line descrption best captures the diverse usage in the real world today: "*Accountability is a concept in ethics with several meanings. It is often used synonymously with such concepts as answerability, responsibility, blameworthiness, liability and other terms associated with the expectation of account-giving."*

Finally, thinking that the apparently endless use of the word in the nonprofit realm might have created a common understanding at least within one sector, I asked nonprofit leaders in several states what "accountability" means to them. Their responses varied widely, from "doing the right thing" and "being transparent" to "being answerable to your stakeholders" and "being ethical." In short, there is no uniform understanding even within the nonprofit sector, where use of the word has been inescapable during the last few years.

So, just as Rost's research led him to write that *"leadership* is a word that has come to mean all things to all people," my review of the term "accountability" leads to a similar conclusion: the simple word "accountability" means different things to different people. Through overuse and misuse, "accountability" seems to have reached buzzword status: a word that, although used ubiquitously and authoritatively, carries a meaning—by both speakers and listeners—that is unclear.

"Transparency" Is Another Buzzword

Similarly, people are calling for more "transparency" within the nonprofit sector, but without a common understanding of what that really means or looks like. Many people interpret "transparency" to mean "open everything to public scrutiny and review." Some use "transparency" as code for "be more ethical." Yet others even intermix buzzwords, using "transparency" to mean "more accountable." In fairness, their confusion is reinforced by the various formal definitions, which range from "allowing the clear transmission of light" to "free from pretense or deceit" and "readily understood; clear."

Danger exists when using terms without a clear understanding of their meaning or how they will be interpreted by others. Telling nonprofits they need to be "transparent" may lead some to conclude that nonprofits must be "see-through," that everything a nonprofit does must be open for public display. While that may sound nice in the abstract to the uninformed, in fact board members have a legal duty to protect certain information as confidential. Indeed, even the IRS recognizes that certain nonprofit information is confidential and that select categories of information may be withheld from general consumption. So before calling for "more transparency" or jumping to certain assumptions when others use the term, people should pause to question what really is meant.

Pillars of Accountability Moves Beyond the Buzzwords

This second edition of *Pillars of Accountability* can help nonprofit leaders look beyond the buzzwords of "accountability" and "transparency" to see the important foundations upon which the terms really are built. Through three mechanisms, *Pillars of Accountability* illustrates what is required to bring appropriate accountability and transparency to nonprofit organizations.

Accountability to the Truth

Through its separate yet interrelated chapters on ethical fundraising, fiscal integrity, strategic risk management, leadership sustainability, and sound employment practices, *Pillars of Accountability* helps readers see the numerous stakeholders to which a nonprofit's board members are accountable, including: donors, other board members, employees, volunteers, clients being served, the public, the law, the organization's governing documents, and the organization as a whole. This cogent book helps new nonprofit leaders avoid falling into the myopic trap of trying to appease just one stakeholder, because the challenge is much larger.

So how can nonprofit leaders balance all of these interests? To whom are they ultimately accountable? Leaders need to appreciate that they are accountable to the truth—an all-important but oft-forgotten concept. In studying the scandals of recent years, I have seen people rationalize their actions by asserting they were doing things out of loyalty to a certain constituency, such as cooking the books to help stockholders or protect the jobs of key employees. By constantly prioritizing loyalty (often to themselves) over the truth, these people found themselves mired in scandals. To avoid future scandals, our society and our leaders need to consciously and purposefully reconnect to the truth. Nonprofit leaders can do this by recognizing that they are accountable to the truth rather than to a single group of stakeholders. This perspective will help thwart damaging short-term rationalizations and provide long-term protection to nonprofits and the communities they serve.

Transparency Requires Clarity, Not Obfuscation

Too often, so-called "experts" tell people what the end results should look like without sharing the required elements on how to make those results possible. For example, saying that a good nonprofit has a strong board with a talented staff may be true, but without sharing any clue about what a strong board and talented staff actually looks like, the description of the overall objective remains abstract and therefore meaningless. That's where the second edition of *Pillars of Accountability* steps into the usual void to add practical clarity.

In this edition, Melanie Herman (executive director of the Nonprofit Risk Management Center) provides important comparisons about what a good nonprofit situation looks like and what a bad one looks like. In so doing, she presents the context for new (as well as experienced) nonprofit leaders to informally assess how well their nonprofits are performing so those leaders may determine whether immediate action is necessary. Also, with its useful check lists, *Pillars of Accountability* supplies a "Goldilocks" level of detail; instead of a "too little" admonition to "go forth and do good things" and rather than a "too much" approach found in a thick legal treatise, this book is "just right" in that it supplies informed, substantive insight for busy people to readily apply in the real world. Finally, while *Pillars of Accountability* offers comprehensive breadth and unique depth, it does not pretend to offer all the answers and openly identifies multiple quality resources for further reference. In sum, in this latest edition, the Nonprofit Risk Management Center provides evidence of the organization's commitment to clear, helpful, and practical service to the nonprofit sector and nonprofit leaders.

Actual Definitions

Finally, unlike other experts who are running around simply repeating the terms "accountability" and "transparency" without explaining what they mean, this book reveals the Center's preferred definitions of those terms. As for the rest of us, while we do not have to adopt the offered definitions beyond this book, I believe it would be a good place for our sector to begin. We need to avoid the empty buzzwords that mean different things to different people. Mere repetition of words with no understanding of their actual meaning will not transform them into magic solutions. In short, to strengthen our sector and our organizations we need to get on the same page. Fortunately for us, the Nonprofit Risk Management Center—with this second edition—has provided the appropriate vehicle to do just that.

—*Tim Delaney, Esq.*

Introduction

There is perhaps no higher calling than serving one's community through the work of a nonprofit organization. Many dedicated community leaders are asked to occupy a place of honor as a member of the board of directors of a nonprofit. Yet many do not realize the weighty responsibilities they will encounter when they agree to volunteer as a board member. Some new board members arrive with an overly optimistic or glossy view of the nonprofit's assets and opportunities. Many report that prior to joining the board, they did not fully appreciate the range of issues and responsibilities which would fall under their purview. Once new board members have put aside the ambitious outlook described in the annual report and taken a hard look at service delivery outcomes, monthly financial statements, and an analysis of funding prospects, they are ready to go to work, but they may still need clarification about just what their scope of work entails. That is the purpose of *Pillars of Accountability*.

Managing a nonprofit in the 21st century offers more challenges than ever before. Nonprofit missions are increasingly bold and ambitious, reliance on costly technology has become the norm, and relationships with key community organizations—from government agencies and local businesses to other nonprofits—have also grown more complex. Something as simple as "borrowing" space from a community church may now require that the nonprofit enter into a contract, provide a certificate of insurance, and substantiate the organization's risk management efforts before it is allowed to occupy the space.

Providing vision and guidance to a nonprofit is further complicated for the board by the public's steadily intensifying scrutiny of nonprofit leadership. This intensified interest, fueled by media reports of wrongdoing by a small number of sector leaders and the growing interest by donors (organizations and individuals alike) in assuring that their chosen charities act responsibly, puts additional pressures and responsibilities on nonprofit leadership. Thus it behooves nonprofit boards to be accountable themselves and to ensure that their organizations are accountable.

Volumes have been written about nonprofit boards' legal responsibilities, ethical dilemmas, governance challenges, and accountability concerns. Much of what has been published during the past decade offers a philosophical or legalistic approach: a board must deliberate with care because the legal *duty of care* requires that it do so. A board should mind that its actions are ethical so that it lives up to the ideals it espouses in the community. A nonprofit board must be accountable to constituencies in order to minimize the risk of dissent, controversy or ultimate failure in achieving the nonprofit's mission. This book acknowledges these ethical and legal imperatives and also offers practical suggestions for targeting accountability weak spots. *Pillars of Accountability* specifically offers advice and suggested action steps in the following areas, which the Nonprofit Risk Management Center believes represent key components of a solid foundation for accountable conduct:

- ❏ Ethical Fundraising
- ❏ Strategic Risk Management
- ❏ Fiscal Integrity
- ❏ Leadership Sustainability

❑   Sound Employment Practices

The Center views improving accountability as an important "to do" item for boards but believes its pursuit should not require a large investment of funds.

This book borrows some of the advice found in the Nonprofit Risk Management Center's free online tool, *Pillars of Accountability*. While the online tool known as "Pillars" is intended to help nonprofit CEOs and other senior managers craft an accountability "to do list," this book is aimed at nonprofit board members. The goal of this publication is to offer a different perspective on some of the ideas held dear by nonprofit leaders, while presenting practical steps that every nonprofit board should consider taking, in order to inch towards the ideal. We purposely choose not to draw an accountability line in the sand and insist that every nonprofit step over it. What constitutes acceptable, appropriate or reasonable action differs so much from one nonprofit to the next. While it may be possible to identify certain conduct as unacceptable in any environment (such as the intentional disregard of the prescribed intent of a donor), most conduct is simply not that easy to classify. What may be unacceptable in one organization (the absence of directors' and officers' liability insurance) may represent a practical reality or thoughtful decision in another.

This book also follows in the footsteps of an earlier publication, *Leaving Nothing to Chance: Achieving Board Accountability Through Risk Management*. In that booklet, published by the National Center for Nonprofit Boards (now known as BoardSource, www.boardsource.org), we outlined 10 steps to achieving greater organizational accountability. *Pillars of Accountability* follows the tradition of this earlier publication by presenting risk management as a foundation for making accountability happen.

Only a nonprofit that is *disinterested in its mission* can afford to ignore the consequences of risk. Unfortunately, the discipline of risk management is too often viewed as a luxury

by nonprofit boards. Representative of board members'
attitudes are:

- ❏ "We're managing risk to some extent, but we just
  don't have time to focus on it due to our ambitious
  capital campaign."

- ❏ "We've been serving young people in this community
  for more than 50 years, and nothing awful has ever
  happened."

- ❏ "Every minute we spend fretting about disaster is one
  less minute spent on planning activities for the
  seniors."

As a result of these attitudes, much risk management is
either lost in a fog of good intentions or buried by self-
confidence. While it is no surprise that an organization that
has never suffered an unfortunate or calamitous surprise would
be reluctant to embrace risk management, it definitely should.

Risk Management as a Launching Pad and Framework

Why position risk management as the foundation for
accountability goal setting and activities? Risk management is
an effective launching pad because when practiced
appropriately it:

- ❏ recognizes the culture, environment, resources and
  challenges facing a particular organization;

- ❏ suggests ways that an organization can gradually
  incorporate changes that increase the safety of its
  assets: people, property, income and reputation;

- ❏ offers a means to identify and address challenges as
  they emerge in an organization; and

- ❏ provides a range of options for addressing the fear,
  anxiety and concern felt by a nonprofit's leaders.

What Is the Board's Role in Risk Management?

Despite the tendency among some nonprofits to treat risk management as an administrative matter, a nonprofit that seeks to incorporate state-of-the-art thinking and practice into its day-to-day operations cannot extract the board of directors from discussion and decision making on the subject of risk. The board's role may be expansive or narrow, tailored to the circumstances, resources and perspective of the organization. No matter how the board fulfills its responsibility for providing leadership in this area, several aspects should be common to all nonprofits. These include the responsibility for making the case for risk management, the duty to model the commitment to risk management, and the board's need to fully understand and appreciate its exposure to liability.

Making the case

Making the case for risk management in a nonprofit begins with the board of directors. A nonprofit board not only establishes policies that govern operations, it models behavior for the organization's paid and volunteer staff, clients, and other constituencies. When a nonprofit's board attaches significance to a particular issue, it is likely that paid staff and other key players will follow suit.

Without sacrificing program goals or a nonprofit's enthusiasm for new activities, the board can and should demonstrate to others that risk management frees up—rather than consumes—resources that can be used to achieve the organization's mission. Through its actions and policies, the board can dispel some of the misconceptions about risk management.

Modeling the commitment

The board has a number of ways to start modeling a commitment to risk management. First, the board can focus on the precautions and steps to be taken to ensure that its own affairs are conducted in a legal and appropriate manner. As the board reviews proposals concerning new activities, it can include safety-related issues in its deliberations. Questions the board might ask include:

❑ What are the risks associated with this activity or program?

❑ Can we conduct this activity or program safely?

❑ If no, what alternative activity would have similar results with an acceptable level of risk?

❑ What resources or actions do we need to take to ensure the safety of staff, clients and the general public?

One of the most important contributions that a nonprofit board makes to the organization's overall risk management effort is to manage its own affairs properly. A board's actions should model its commitment to excellent management that includes risk management. When the board takes its responsibilities seriously, others will follow the board's lead.

Understanding board liability

Every nonprofit board has specific legal duties of care, loyalty, and obedience. The *duty of care* asks a director to be reasonably informed, participate in decisions, and to act in good faith and with the care of an ordinarily prudent person in similar circumstances. Ways to assess a board member's commitment include asking if the person participates actively in decisions, attends meetings, uses independent judgment, and seeks reliable information to make informed decisions.

The *duty of loyalty* requires that a board member put the interests of the organization first, ahead of any personal interest or the interest of another party or entity. Loyalty issues usually arise from actual or perceived conflicts of interest, appropriation of a corporate opportunity (a member engages in a transaction that may be of interest to the organization), and breaches of confidentiality. Each nonprofit should have written and enforced policies on conflict of interest and confidentiality.

Board obedience relates to the need to act in accordance with the nonprofit's mission and all applicable laws and regulations. A common allegation of *board malfeasance* is that the board is not staying true to the organization's mission and purpose. Remember that in addition to the board itself, many external entities regulate and monitor nonprofits closely to ensure that they maintain their charitable functions.

To meet a board's legal duties and manage the risks associated with governing an organization the directors must be committed to being effective members. The board can enhance its ability to act appropriately by providing its members with information and guidance. One tool is a manual that includes basic documents and information on the organization's history, structure and activities. Another tool is a board orientation program to bring new board members up-to-date quickly. Board minutes serve to inform new members and to document the board's actions. These and other activities will help board members meet their responsibilities and be accountable to members and stakeholders.

In addition to following the rules that guide its operations, an accountable board meets in an environment characterized by a culture of candor. Each board member must feel comfortable raising difficult issues for discussion (e.g. "Will this new program truly further our mission, or are we pursuing this opportunity due to the associated revenue?" or "Is the figure proposed for client fees realistic given our history of declining demand for services?"). The opposite environment—where board members feel that asking tough questions reflects disloyalty to the organization and its staff—is poisonous for an organization seeking to achieve greater accountability.

Risk Management Checklist for Board Operations

- ❑ Does the board keep thorough, accurate records? Do the board meeting minutes document every corporate action taken? Are dissenting views and votes reflected?

- ❑ Do the minutes reflect which directors were in attendance?

- ❑ Does the board have operating procedures, either outlined in the nonprofit's Bylaws or elsewhere?

- ❑ Does the board explore options before arriving at a decision?

- ❑ Do board deliberations reflect a "culture of candor," an environment where board members feel they are permitted and encouraged to ask difficult questions and discuss controversial topics facing the organization?

- ❑ Are attendance policies in place and enforced for board members who fail to participate?

- ❑ Do board members stay informed about the organization's activities? Are background materials provided in advance of each meeting? Do board members ask questions and seek clarification on matters before them?

- ❑ Does the board have a conflict of interest policy? Is the policy followed?

- ❑ Is adequate notice of meetings provided in accordance with the Bylaws?

- ❑ Are board members elected in accordance with procedures outlined in the Bylaws?

As indicated previously, this book explores five pillars of accountability: Ethical Fundraising, Strategic Risk Management, Fiscal Integrity, Leadership Sustainability, and Sound Employment Practices.

These Pillars provide a foundation for preserving and protecting the integrity of your organization. We hope this book inspires your board to sharpen its collective pencil on the issue of accountability. As you read the chapters ahead, consider what goals are appropriate given your circumstances and resources. Take a closer look at your accountability goals and the steps you can reasonably take to achieve them.

Chapter 1
Ethical Fundraising

I n all but rare instances, an effective fund-raising strategy is
essential to sustaining a nonprofit organization. With the
exception of the nonprofit that has a multi-year government
contract or substantial income from an enormous endowment,
most nonprofits and nonprofit boards find themselves
continually immersed in a hunt for funds. Potential sources of
funding include private foundations, government agencies and
private businesses. The greatest potential for resources remains
with individual donors whose donations still represent the
largest share of charitable giving in the United States.

Ethical dilemmas in fundraising are almost as common as
ambitious fund-raising goals. Here are just a few examples of
some of the practical, day-to-day dilemmas that crop up when
nonprofit board members and staff embark on the virtuous
task of fundraising:

❑ *Going Where the Money Is*—Board members may
suggest that the organization make adjustments to its
vision and mission in order to gain access to funds.
Why not expand the day-care center to serve adults as
well as children since government agencies seem to
have funding available for adult day care?

❑ *Promises, Promises*—Donors are as different as the
projects their contributions support. Yet the desire for
recognition and some level of control remains and

should be anticipated. How does the board respond when the largest donor to a capital campaign insists that the firm that employs his son be designated project architect? How should the board separate acceptable from inappropriate strings attached to funding commitments? What action is in order when the board realizes it has made a promise it cannot or should not keep?

❑ *Everything Changes*—Most grant proposals attempt to paint a picture of the world as the nonprofit sees it (now) and hopes to see it in the future. Great attention is paid to the contrast between what is now and what can be—with the donor's support. While writing talent and management skills may be plentiful in the nonprofit sector, psychic ability is not. Sometimes things do not turn out the way that the nonprofit thought they would. What should the board do when this occurs in the midst of a grant-funded initiative? What level of disclosure is required and at what risk? How can the nonprofit inform a funder about a change in plans without jeopardizing the funding and the ability of the nonprofit to continue?

❑ *Reining in Dollars*—To successfully raise funds, most nonprofits rely on the talents, persuasive ability and personal networks of volunteer board members. To some extent success may be driven by the degree to which board members are allowed to "do their thing." What responsibility does the nonprofit bear for overseeing the fund-raising efforts, promises, commitments and activities of its fund-raising agents? Do the leaders of an accountable nonprofit worry about the promises and commitments made by persons acting on the organization's behalf? Are persons who solicit funds on the nonprofit's behalf cautioned about appropriate and inappropriate promises and commitments? Is this guidance also provided to a fundraiser who is being paid to represent the organization?

❑ *Step Right Up, Sign at the X*—By the time the grant agreement letter arrives, the proceeds of a new grant have already been spent—perhaps not literally, but in the minds of the professional staff. When a careful review of the letter reveals conditions previously unknown to the staff, it is both the time and place to thoughtfully consider whether the nonprofit can meet the grant conditions and therefore accept the funds. But in many respects it is too late for this analysis. The likelihood of not accepting new funds because of onerous grant conditions is next to nil for most nonprofits. What is more likely is the tendency for these contracts to be treated like other contracts and hastily signed by the nonprofit.

❑ *When Silence Isn't Golden*—Partnering with another nonprofit or for-profit to sell a produce or service to an organization's clientele may yield dollars for the bottom line. But when the buyer is kept in the dark about the percentage of the purchase price that actually benefits the charity, he or she may unwittingly consider the entire purchase a tax-deductible contribution. Disclosing the "value" of the donation is essential to transparency in your fund-raising efforts and necessary to keep both the nonprofit and the donor/buyer out of hot water.

❑ *The Slight Exaggeration*—Conveying a nonprofit's accomplishments in the best possible light is an important aspect of fund-raising strategy. The availability of online funder research tools makes it easier than in the past to determine a funder's likes, dislikes, desires and requirements. And computer technology makes it a snap to incorporate these preferences into our funding proposals. But what responsibility does a nonprofit bear with regard to accurately representing its programs and accomplishments? An ethical fund-raising program never blurs the distinction between current programs and accomplishments versus aspirations for the future. It is never appropriate to mislead donors or potential donors about the status of your nonprofit.

What Does an Ethical Fund-Raising Program Look Like?

An organization that has achieved the goal of raising all funds in an ethical manner might have some of the following characteristics:

❑ Before their gifts are accepted, donors are fully informed about the way in which funds will be used.

❑ Donors who offer gifts that principally benefit the donor, versus the nonprofit, are politely turned down.

❑ Grant agreements are perused carefully before they are signed, and any questions or concerns that arise from these contracts are discussed with the government or foundation program officer before the nonprofit signs the contract.

❑ Gift agreements are used to clarify either that the gift is restricted in some way or that the charity may use the gift at its discretion.

❑ Anytime the plans described in a funding proposal must change while a funded project is under way, the nonprofit promptly contacts the funder and requests an opportunity to brief the funder and request approval for modifications to the scope of work. Such approval is obtained before work proceeds in a direction that deviates from the original funding proposal.

❑ If a nonprofit can't use a gift in accordance with the donor's restriction, the gift is returned unless the donor gives permission for an alternative use.

❑ Information on the nonprofit's donors is carefully guarded to substantially reduce the risk that personal information about a donor might be read by someone without authority to access that information.

- ❏ Details on grant expenditures are meticulously maintained, and staff is able to generate current reports on all open grants.

- ❏ Complete narrative and financial reports are submitted on time to each funder that requires these reports. An annual report on the nonprofit is submitted to donors that do not require grant-specific reports.

What Does an Unethical Program Look Like?

A nonprofit whose fundraising does not achieve a passing grade might have some of the following characteristics:

- ❏ Fund-raising consultants are largely responsible for conducting solicitations on the nonprofit's behalf, and their compensation is directly tied to the amount they raise.

- ❏ Solicitations and proposals to prospective funders offer only vague statements about the nonprofit's current financial status, past success and accomplishments, or its intentions with respect to the use of new donations.

- ❏ Donors sometimes, but not always, receive acknowledgements of their support.

- ❏ Records of grant expenditures are maintained in a haphazard fashion.

- ❏ A significant percentage of the nonprofit's revenue is spent on fundraising and administrative costs, with less than half of each donated dollar devoted to programs.

- ❏ Accounts are padded to spend down grant monies.

- ❏ Money from anyone for anything is accepted, no questions asked.

- ❏ Funds from one project are used to cover a project that is over budget.

- The nonprofit sells its donor list to earn extra revenue without first disclosing its intent to do so to donors/prospective donors and providing an "opt-out" option.

- If plans change, the funder is told after the fact, because it is easier to ask for forgiveness than for permission.

- The fund-raising contract is given to a board member's spouse who is rumored to have raised buckets of money for nonprofits elsewhere.

The Board's Ethical Fund-Raising "To Do" List

This section offers a list of possible steps that a nonprofit board might pursue in order to address weaknesses in the ethical foundation of the nonprofit's fund-raising efforts. In addition to selecting an action step, it is vital to identify a target date for completion and the lead board or staff member for the task. Review the list and check those that are suitable for your nonprofit.

Fund-raising Personnel

- Review current contractual relationships with contract fundraisers. Has the nonprofit made its expectations and requirements clear? Is sufficient training provided to contractors to enable them to perform adequately? Has anything happened in the past to suggest that the nonprofit should be doing more to orient contractors to its culture and requirements?

- Is each person who solicits funds on the nonprofit's behalf tuned into the ethical issues that surround fundraising? (Remember to consider paid staff, board members and other volunteers, and contract fundraisers.) Do they understand that they must be accountable to the organization, as well as to the donors? Is the training provided to fundraisers sufficient to protect the organization?

❑ Verify that all professional, paid fundraisers are registered with the state as required. If not, require that fundraisers register in accordance with state law.

❑ Determine whether the nonprofit prepares adequately for turnover in its fund-raising staff. Is the nonprofit overly dependent on one or more fundraisers, whose departure could jeopardize the organization's financial picture? What strategy is appropriate to shore up the staffing of the fund-raising function so that it can withstand personnel changes?

Fund-Raising Expenses

❑ Evaluate the nonprofit's fund-raising expense-to-outcomes ratio to determine how much the organization spends on fundraising compared to the dollars it raises for mission-related programming. Examine each fund-raising strategy employed by the nonprofit to determine ratios for each project—direct mail, annual dinner, special event and others. Which strategies have the lowest ratios and which have the highest? Does the nonprofit stay within the 1:3 ratio (no more than 25 percent of donated dollars are spent on pure fund-raising expenses versus programs) for all fundraising? If not, what changes are in order?

Accountability to Funders/Donors

❑ Evaluate the nonprofit's track record and reputation with its principal funders. Does the nonprofit regularly adhere to funder requirements and deadlines? If not, what changes are required to ensure greater accountability on the part of the staff members who are assigned responsibility for meeting funder paperwork requirements?

❑ Evaluate the process used to ensure that donor restrictions, requests and special needs are addressed in a timely fashion. What grade has the nonprofit earned with respect to fulfilling promises, communicating difficulties and challenges openly, and maintaining lines of communication with donors? What is the nonprofit's track record with regard to acknowledging its failure to achieve campaign or project goals or meet other deliverables specified in grant proposals or funding requests?

❑ Review the process used to document and track grant requirements. Are reporting requirements assigned to key staff members who are held accountable?

❑ Review marketing and solicitation letters to make certain that they are clear and unambiguous about the manner in which donations will be spent—for operating expenses, to fund cash donations to needy clients, to support the purchase of new equipment for a recreation center, or for other purposes. Make certain that all written fund-raising materials are accurate and free from any potentially misleading information.

❑ Review written materials (e.g. letters, brochures, flyers) soliciting funds to make certain that they contain contact information that will enable potential donors to contact the nonprofit if they have questions or concerns about the appeal.

❑ Review all current fund-raising materials and campaign letters for the single purpose of determining the specific ways in which they may misrepresent your programs and services. Consider the impression these materials could give a typical reader who is unfamiliar with your nonprofit. For example, does the literature suggest the nonprofit is a direct service provider when the organization is actually a funder, a resource to direct service providers or something else? Does the literature suggest the nonprofit serves families when it is serving only children or another population subset? Do any of the campaign materials discuss activities in the present tense that were conducted or concluded years ago? Identify the items that need to be updated to ensure that unfamiliar readers will get an accurate impression of services.

- ❑ Review all current fund-raising materials and campaign letters to determine whether they accurately explain how the funds generated through the campaign will be spent. Identify areas where a reader might be misled about how his or her donation will be spent.

- ❑ Update the language in all fund-raising materials and letters to ensure that a clear picture is presented about how the organization will use the funds provided in response to the campaign or outreach.

- ❑ Design a process for ensuring that before letters and brochures and fund-raising materials are printed they are reviewed to make certain that (1) information on the programs and services of the nonprofit is accurate and up to date; and (2) references to how campaign monies will be spent are accurate.

- ❑ Determine the identity of the person (and a back up) in the nonprofit who is responsible for acknowledging gifts and donations. Is the individual held accountable for providing timely acknowledgments?

- ❑ Verify that written, express permission has been obtained from any and all persons (clients and others) featured in fund-raising materials used by the nonprofit (e.g. photographs, quoted text).

- ❑ Determine the nonprofit's process for responding to a donor request for a receipt that exceeds the value of the goods or services provided to the nonprofit. Make certain that key personnel understand that if there is a conflict between a donor's desires and legal requirements, the nonprofit must always substantiate gifts in accordance with legal requirements.

Gift Acceptance Policy

- ❑ Determine whether the nonprofit has a current gift acceptance policy that provides a framework for determining whether an incoming gift meets the nonprofit's needs and any relevant restrictions (e.g., no gifts of real property or no gifts from the tobacco industry). Has the policy ever been invoked as the basis for rejecting a gift? If so, what were the consequences of that action? How does the organization communicate with donors concerning the suitability of a gift: Is the rejection communicated by the highest development official in the organization or assigned to an administrative staff member?

❑ If no gift acceptance policy currently exists, create a diagram of the process of soliciting and receiving corporate and individual donations in the nonprofit. Identify the logical place where an appropriate staff member or volunteer could conduct a review of donor requirements and determine whether the nonprofit is in position to meet the requirements.

Handling Donor Requests and Complaints

❑ Review any unusual requests from corporate and individual donors made during the past five years, including the nonprofit's response. Was the nonprofit's response to each request appropriate? Review the process your nonprofit uses to reject an inappropriate gift, or one accompanied by strings the organization cannot accept. Is the process effective?

❑ Review past instances where post-contribution donor requests were granted and denied. Determine if the nonprofit's response has been consistent. If not, identify what measures are necessary to ensure consistency in the future. Some of the items that may be useful in evaluating these past requests include: name of donor, nature of request, estimated cost of fulfilling request, staff member who made decision, what alternatives if any were considered, and fallout from the decision made, if any.

❑ Identify the process used for handling donor complaints. Review complaints from donors during the past five years. Indicate the circumstances surrounding the complaint and the action taken by the nonprofit in response. What changes are warranted in the way that complaints are handled?

Leadership Awareness

❏ Review the organization's Web site, letterhead and sample funding appeals to determine whether the identity of the board of directors is readily available to prospective donors. Is the current board list readily available and used in fundraising? What changes are required to make certain that fund-raising efforts consistently disclose the identity of the leaders of the nonprofit?

Responding to Financial Inquiries

❏ Determine whether the nonprofit has designated a single point of contact (such as the chief financial officer) for inquiries about obtaining financial information on the organization. Determine in what format financial statements will be provided upon request. For example, some organizations may refer persons making inquiries to the most recent Form 990 available on the nonprofit's Web site or at www.guidestar.org. Other nonprofits may release copies of audited annual financial statements upon request, while others may prepare special financial reports for release. What is the organization's track record of compliance with such requests? Is there any evidence that requests for financial information have been denied or the organization has sought to avoid responding?

❏ Examine the financial statements and reports the nonprofit provides to donors. Determine whether they include the amount of donations spent on actual programs and services. If it is not clear what percentage of donor dollars are devoted to service delivery, determine the most effective way to present this information. Some organizations pursue a strategy to ensure that a large percentage of donated funds support service delivery, perhaps using funds from product sales or other miscellaneous revenue resources to pay for rent, utilities, administrative staff and other overhead. Others allocate overhead expenses proportionately across all projects, including those supported by grants and donations. Keep in mind the importance donors attach to your ability to spend a high percentage of donations on service delivery. One prominent publisher reports on "Top Charities" and "Charities to Avoid" using the percentage an organization spends on services as the principal rating tool.

Donor Communication

❑ Consider how the nonprofit could periodically monitor fund-raising efforts to ensure that fundraisers are following the organization's requirements such as recording telephone solicitations or conducting random follow-up surveys with donors to inquire about their interactions with staff, volunteers or paid solicitors, and others.

❑ Identify steps the nonprofit could take to actively encourage donors to ask questions. For example, posting a list of "Frequently Asked Questions From Donors" on your Web site, or adding a statement to fund-raising scripts, such as "Do you have any questions about the organization you'd like to ask?"

❑ Identify questions that past donors have asked or questions that you think might be asked in the future, and compile these into a Frequently Asked Questions document that you can distribute to fund-raising personnel.

Protecting Donor Privacy

❑ Verify that the organization has an effective process for allowing donors to request that their names not appear on donors lists or be sold or shared with persons or organizations outside the nonprofit's fund development office. Test the "opt out" mechanism for donors to ensure that it works as intended.

- ❏ Identify whether there have been any cases where a donor's privacy has been breached, despite your precautions. Determine the causes of the breach and whether steps have been taken to prevent another breach. Could the same breach occur again? What should be done to notify donors of possible breaches?

- ❏ Identify the specific steps taken to guard donor privacy. For example:

  - ■ Using a secure Web site to process donations by credit card;
  - ■ Using encryption technology to store credit card numbers in your database;
  - ■ Adopting a policy that prohibits the sale of your donor list to any third party;
  - ■ Training all staff on the importance of not disclosing donor information and addressing hypothetical disclosure situations;
  - ■ Training all staff on the safeguards your organization intends to implement.

- ❏ Determine whether all paid staff, volunteers and contractors who need to be familiar with the list of donor privacy rules and requirements understand each requirement. Do they understand the importance of adhering to these policies and procedures? What steps are required, such as scheduling a periodic briefing, to remind the nonprofit's staff about the importance and mechanics of these safeguards?

Donor Anonymity

- ❏ Determine whether the nonprofit provides an adequate opportunity for donors to request anonymity and whether appropriate steps are taken to meet these requests.

- ❏ Examine the internal process used for removing someone from your solicitation lists. Identify possible cracks in the system whereby the name might not be removed sufficiently to avoid calls, mailings, etc. Address the "cracks" to increase responsiveness to donors.

From communicating openly with funders about challenges that arise during a grant period to ensuring that requests for donor anonymity are met, an ethical fund-raising program is both dynamic and complex. A nonprofit that strives for the highest levels of ethical conduct in its fundraising must be well-organized, vigilant, and responsive to issues and concerns that arise along the fund-raising path. Examining and establishing systems and processes to address the issues discussed in this chapter represent a sound investment for a nonprofit. While each organization must determine what course is appropriate—given its organizational maturity, the relationship between board and staff and the division of labor among board and staff—attention to the area of fundraising is an essential component of enlightened and effective board service.

Resources on Ethical Fundraising

The Nonprofit Risk Management Center urges readers to consult the texts, Web sites, and organizations listed on the next two pages for additional insights on the subject of ethical fundraising.

No Strings Attached: Untangling the Risks of Fundraising & Collaboration, published by the Nonprofit Risk Management Center and available at **www.nonprofitrisk.org.**

Association of Fundraising Professionals—AFP seeks to foster development and growth of fundraising professionals committed to preserving and enhancing philanthropy, and requires members to adhere to a professional code of ethical standards and practices. **www.AFPnet.org.**

BBB Wise Giving Alliance—A merger of the National Charities Information Bureau and the Council of Better Business Bureaus' Foundation and its Philanthropic Advisory Service. The site includes 20 voluntary Alliance charity standards. The Alliance reports on nationally soliciting charitable organizations that are the subject of donor inquiries. These reports include an evaluation of the subject charity in relation to the voluntary *BBB charity standards.*

The BBB Wise Giving Alliance Standards for Charity Accountability were developed to assist donors in making sound giving decisions and to foster public confidence in charitable organizations. The standards seek to encourage fair and honest solicitation practices, to promote ethical conduct by charitable organizations and to advance support of philanthropy. **www.give.org**

Independent Sector—Independent Sector works to strengthen, empower, and partner with nonprofit and philanthropic organizations. Visit the accountability section of the organization's Web site which offers "tools, resources, and links to help nonprofits and foundations improve practice and self regulation, as well as information on proposals being considered by policymakers to strengthen legislative and regulatory oversight." **www.independentsector.org**

Internet Nonprofit Center—This Web site features a link to the Unified Registration Statement. "The URS represents an effort to consolidate the information and data requirements of all states that require registration of nonprofit organizations performing charitable solicitations within their jurisdictions. The effort is organized by the *National Association of State Charities Officials* and the *National Association of Attorneys General,* and is one part of the Standardized Reporting Project, whose aim is to standardize, simplify, and economize compliance under the states' solicitation laws." **www.nonprofits.org** and **www.multistatefiling.org**

National Association of State Charities Officials—NASCO members are employees of state and federal agencies that regulate charitable trusts, fundraising, and nonprofit hospitals in the U.S. The NASCO Web site provides general information to the public, including contact information and news updates for compliance with state and federal laws regarding charitable solicitations. **www.NASCOnet.org**

The Foundation Center—Founded in 1956, The Foundation Center is the nation's leading authority on philanthropy and is dedicated to serving grantseekers, grantmakers, researchers, policymakers, the media, and the general public. The Center believes that "Transparency and accountability are key to earning the public trust." **www.fdncenter.org**

The Donor Bill of Rights

The Donor Bill of Rights was created by the American Association of Fund Raising Counsel (AAFRC), Association for Healthcare Philanthropy (AHP), the Association of Fundraising Professionals (AFP), and the Council for Advancement and Support of Education (CASE). It has been endorsed by numerous organizations. It is available online at www.afpnet.org.

Philanthropy is based on voluntary action for the common good. It is a tradition of giving and sharing that is primary to the quality of life. To ensure that philanthropy merits the respect and trust of the general public, and that donors and prospective donors can have full confidence in the nonprofit organizations and causes they are asked to support, we declare that all donors have these rights:

I.   To be informed of the organization's mission, of the way the organization intends to use donated resources, and of its capacity to use donations effectively for their intended purposes.

II. To be informed of the identity of those serving on the organization's governing board, and to expect the board to exercise prudent judgment in its stewardship responsibilities.

III. To have access to the organization's most recent financial statements.

IV. To be assured their gifts will be used for the purposes for which they were given.

V.   To receive appropriate acknowledgement and recognition.

VI. To be assured that information about their donation is handled with respect and with confidentiality to the extent provided by law.

VII. To expect that all relationships with individuals representing organizations of interest to the donor will be professional in nature.

VIII. To be informed whether those seeking donations are volunteers, employees of the organization or hired solicitors.

IX. To have the opportunity for their names to be deleted from mailing lists that an organization may intend to share.

X.   To feel free to ask questions when making a donation and to receive prompt, truthful and forthright answers.

Chapter 2
Strategic Risk Management

The discipline of risk management provides both a framework for this book and the subject matter for this chapter. A nonprofit board that disregards how the organization *takes* and *manages* risk places the mission of the nonprofit in jeopardy. Risk management is not simply "an administrative matter," as some nonprofit leaders have wrongfully concluded. The risks an organization takes go to the heart of its mission and prospects for survival and success. This chapter examines strategic risk management from a different perspective than a book directed to management or line staff. While the latter publication might admonish staff working with hazardous materials to wear appropriate protective gear, this chapter emphasizes concerns that require the board's apt and ongoing attention.

For What Purpose?

What is the purpose of engaging a nonprofit board in risk management? What might the board's diligence in this area yield for the nonprofit? There are many ways to describe the goals or mission of risk management and the unique qualities and challenges facing individual organizations warrant specific emphasis in one area or another. Here are three goals that would be appropriate in any nonprofit:

Goal 1 *Establish and support a deeply ingrained risk management sensibility and accountability and greater awareness and visibility of risk.* The nonprofit that has achieved this goal embraces risk taking as well as risk management, and does so in a thoughtful, not haphazard, manner.

Goal 2 *Create and foster awareness of and focus on the most critical risks facing the nonprofit,* including upside risks that benefit the nonprofit's mission and downside risks that impair mission fulfillment. The nonprofit that has achieved this goal directs proportionate resources to the risks it faces and views risk expansively, as representing both positive and negative outcomes.

Goal 3 *Reduce surprise.* A universal goal of risk management is to reduce surprises. While most humans relish an occasional "good surprise," even good surprises can throw effective nonprofits off their game. So risk management is a discipline that allows an organization to look more carefully at the future and plan for a range of possibilities. In doing so the organization reduces the chance of surprise and increases the opportunity to devote limited resources to their highest use.

What Does a Nonprofit That Manages Risk Strategically Look Like?

❏ The nonprofit's board is clear about and can articulate the organization's priority upside *and* downside risks.

❏ The board views risk taking as essential to mission fulfillment.

❏ The board appreciates the nonprofit's governance risks and has taken steps to make certain that its key governing documents and tools are up to date.

❏ The board understands the relationship between risk management and insurance, including the role of insurance as a risk-financing option and the board recognizes that the nonprofit faces insurable, as well as uninsurable, risks.

❑ The board conducts its own evaluation of the adequacy of the nonprofit's insurance coverage and accepts responsibility for understanding how the nonprofit finances risk and protects assets from catastrophic loss.

❑ The organization values and seeks independence in its relationship with outside advisers, including the nonprofit's legal counsel, financial advisor and insurance professional.

❑ The board understands and embraces its role in the organization's overall commitment to integrate risk management into the culture and operations of the nonprofit.

What Does a Nonprofit That Has Ignored Strategic Risk Management Look Like?

❑ The nonprofit is frequently in "crisis management mode," requiring staff and board members to "extinguish fires" that were unexpected.

❑ The nonprofit sees risk in the negative sense only— little or no time is devoted to considering upside risks.

❑ The nonprofit receives advice on insurance and safety matters from a board member who also acts as the organization's insurance agent.

❑ The board and staff lack a clear understanding of the nonprofit's critical risks or the strategies most appropriate for managing those risks.

❑ The board and senior management consider any discussion of risk to be a waste of time and money that could be better spent on raising funds, developing new programs, or recruiting volunteers.

- [ ] Board members get bored with the big picture; they are more interested in running day-to-day operations.

- [ ] The board views insurance as a cure-all that will cover injuries and accidents—should they happen.

- [ ] No one has been assigned responsibility for tracking and evaluating risk issues, such as insurance premiums, accident rates, lost-work days, medical costs, and other data that would show trends and patterns.

The Board's Strategic Risk Management "To Do" List

This section offers a list of possible steps that a nonprofit board might pursue in order to address weaknesses in the nonprofit's existing risk management efforts. In addition to selecting an action step, it is vital to identify a target date for completion and the lead board or staff member for the task. Review the list and check those that are suitable to your nonprofit.

Risk Management Committee

- [ ] If a Risk Management Committee does not currently exist, determine whether there is an existing committee that could be re-purposed or broadened to take on risk management issues, or whether it makes more sense to create a separate committee for this purpose.

- [ ] Determine the appropriate makeup of the committee. Are there essential positions versus flexible positions on the committee? For example, some nonprofits determine that having the organization's legal and insurance advisors on the committee is absolutely necessary, but the participation of various staff members can change.

- [ ] Establish an appropriate mission and work program for the risk management committee. What tasks will it take on? How often will it meet? What are the immediate or top priority assignments for the committee? In some nonprofits a top priority might be overseeing the bidding process for the nonprofit's insurance program.

❑   Consider the reporting structure and format for the risk management committee. How will the decisions or actions of the committee be reported to the board and how often?

Governance Risks

The legal structure and operation of a nonprofit affects the possibility of suffering a loss or achieving a gain. Disregard for the organization's mission or not following the bylaws can have negative consequences.

❑   Determine if the nonprofit's articles of incorporation are reviewed periodically to ensure both compliance with state law and concurrency with the organization's mission and purpose. If necessary, determine the steps required to amend the articles.

❑   Determine if the nonprofit's bylaws are reviewed periodically to ensure that they reflect current circumstances and operations. If the bylaws require updating, establish a schedule to bring this important governing tool up to date.

❑   Confirm that the nonprofit's bylaws contain a provision indemnifying board members. When an organization agrees to indemnify its board members it promises to pay the directors' legal costs (usually both defense expenses and any settlements or judgments) from claims arising from board service. Keep in mind that indemnification is a hollow promise unless the nonprofit has a financing strategy in place (with respect to claims against board members, the most affordable strategy may be a directors' and officers' liability insurance policy).

❑   Review the organization's current conflict of interest policy. Does the policy require that board members complete and sign an annual disclosure statement declaring any known conflicts and agreeing to comply with the policy? Has the policy been followed since its adoption? If not, what steps are required to ensure compliance?

❑ If the nonprofit does not have a conflict of interest policy in place, establishing such a policy should be a top priority. The policy should cover senior managers as well as the board. Sample policies are available from various management assistance organizations, including the Nonprofit Risk Management Center, BoardSource and various state associations of nonprofits (see www.NCNA.org).

❑ Consider the adequacy of the orientation materials provided to new board members. Does the board manual or orientation packet include the kinds of information the board needs to fulfill its legal duties?

❑ Consider whether the board training session or orientation ensures that board members are prepared for their service. Does the orientation provide an opportunity for experienced board members to share their insights and coach the new members in fulfilling their board duties?

❑ Consider whether the board has committed to evaluating and improving its performance as a responsible, accountable and effective governing body. Does it periodically evaluate its performance and adopt a work plan to address any weaknesses? If not, what steps are required to add board self-assessment to the annual work plan?

Legal Compliance

Nonprofits are subject to oversight and regulation by numerous entities—the IRS, states attorneys general, federal, state, and local laws and umbrella organizations. In addition, every nonprofit voluntarily submits to enforceable legal obligations through the contracts it enters into. The range of requirements depends upon the nature of the organization and the services provided. Even small nonprofits have numerous legal requirements.

Some experts argue that legal compliance is distinct from risk management because legal compliance addresses things a nonprofit must do in all cases, while risk management is often aspirational. This argument certainly has merit, yet most nonprofits in the U.S. view achieving legal compliance as part of their overall commitment to risk management. Whether the subject is treated as a separate discipline or incorporated into a nonprofit's risk management program depends on the culture and history of the organization. The most important message for the board is that the governing body of a nonprofit cannot discharge its legal duty of care without addressing the issue of how the nonprofit achieves compliance with relevant laws and regulations.

❑ Determine if the nonprofit has designated an individual inside or outside the nonprofit with responsibility for monitoring legal compliance. Is this designation appropriate given the current needs and circumstances facing the nonprofit? Is the nonprofit's current legal counsel an effective advisor to and advocate for the organization? Does the nonprofit's advisor possess the expertise required by the organization? If not, what course of action is required to identify and appoint a suitable advisor?

❑ Identify the process that has been established for ensuring that the board is kept abreast of legal developments that may influence its decision-making and governance activities. Is this process adequate or does it require updating?

❑ Determine whether the board requires additional training, information or support in order to understand and appreciate the legal requirements facing the nonprofit and the organization's strategy for achieving legal compliance.

Risk Financing Strategy

The board is responsible for financial oversight of the organization as well as ensuring that the organization has adequate resources to achieve its mission. One way to safeguard the organization's financial assets is to have the proper insurance in place. The board should first establish a strategy that guides the organization's risk financing, including its insurance purchasing decisions. A risk financing strategy describes the nonprofit's philosophy about paying for losses and the tools that the organization intends to use to pay for losses.

❑ Consider developing a risk financing strategy. For example:

> *[Name of Nonprofit] is committed to protecting its financial and human assets to the greatest extent possible. [Name of Nonprofit] will seek to eliminate or reduce as much as practicable the conditions, activities, and practices that cause insurable losses. The organization will purchase insurance to provide indemnity for catastrophic losses and will decide, based on an analysis of the best interests of the organization, to either insure or retain those risks not considered of major importance to mission-critical operations and financial well-being. The board will receive an annual insurance stewardship report summarizing its insurance program, any significant losses and any changes made to the program during the prior year.*

❑ Review the nonprofit's risk financing strategy to make certain that the division of labor between the staff and the board is clear. For example:

> *To safeguard the assets and resources of [Name of Nonprofit], the organization will purchase insurance for those insurable risks of major importance to mission-critical operations and the financial health of the organization. It is the executive director's responsibility to oversee the organization's insurance program and provide an annual insurance report to the board.*

Insurance Awareness

When asked about the adequacy of their nonprofit's insurance coverage, some board members report that they have received assurances from the organization's broker that the coverage meets the nonprofit's needs. Other board members express concern that the *insurance program*—a term referring to the collection of coverages purchased by an organization—may not be adequate. Responsibility for the fiscal health of a nonprofit and its mission are important facets of board responsibility. While professional staff members and outside advisors can provide invaluable assistance to the board, the board should never view the subject of insurance as falling completely outside the board's territory. As is true with other areas of operations, when a nonprofit matures day-to-day responsibility gradually shifts to professional staff and paid advisors. However, the board should periodically consider its understanding of the insurance program and make certain it has the tools it needs to makes its own assessment of adequacy.

❑ Determine the board's comfort level with the nonprofit's insurance program. Does each board member have a basic understanding of the coverages purchased by the organization?

❑ If the board is unfamiliar with the package of policies that protect the nonprofit from catastrophic financial loss, what information, resources, or education about the program are required to bring the board up to date?

❑ If the board has a strong, working knowledge of the nonprofit's insurance program, are there periodic reports and presentations which highlight changes, challenges or new developments?

❑ What concerns have board members raised about the nonprofit's insurance program? Have these concerns been addressed to the board's satisfaction? If not, what additional help might be required to obtain timely answers that will facilitate informed decision-making?

Independent Insurance Advisor

When a nonprofit's insurance advisor also serves on the board, various difficulties can ensue due to the lack of independence of this key advisor. The following steps are appropriate for nonprofits that find themselves in this difficult situation.

☐ Identify ways that the insurance professional could be supportive of the organization without serving on the board or other governing body. For example, perhaps he or she can serve on the risk management committee, or another committee involving nonboard members.

☐ Discuss with the insurance professional what would happen in the event a dispute ensued about the services he or she provided.

☐ Determine whether the insurance professional's board service outweighs his or her professional service to the organization, and whether a new advisor should be sought or the insurance professional should simply step down from the board or not seek re-election.

Finding a competent, helpful insurance advisor is an important step in protecting the mission as well as the financial assets of a nonprofit.

☐ If your nonprofit does not currently have an insurance advisor (broker, agent or consultant), contact a minimum of three nonprofit agencies and request contact information for each agency's insurance professional. Consider three nonprofits that provide similar services (e.g. mentoring, health, recreation) or three nonprofits in the community where the nonprofit works on a regular basis. This process is similar to finding a primary care physician or dentist upon moving to a new community—start your search by seeking recommendations from friends and colleagues.

☐ Check out the Web sites of the insurance professionals that sister or neighboring organizations are using. Do the sites indicate that the agency/ broker specializes in nonprofits? If not, is it clear from the sites that the professionals have substantive experience working with nonprofit clients?

❑ Assuming that the nonprofits you contacted were pleased overall with the service they are receiving, contact each of the three recommended insurance professionals and inquire whether they are accepting new customers. Request a list of nonprofit client references from each.

❑ Contact the references of each prospective insurance professional/provider.

Consider asking:

■ How long have you been a client of the agency/broker?
■ How would you describe the service you have received?
■ What advice would you offer to a new client of this agent/broker?
■ Have you worked with the agent/broker on both the sales side of the process as well as an actual claim?
■ If yes, was the agent/broker responsive when you filed a claim?
■ Do you have any reservations about recommending your agent/broker to another nonprofit?

Risk View

❑ Consider the board's view on risk taking and risk management. Does the current view support or impede mission fulfillment? For example, some nonprofit boards take an overly conservative view that may prevent the organization from seizing opportunities. Other boards endorse new activities without sufficient consideration of the attendant risks.

❑ If the board's "risk view" requires updating, what resources are required to help the board reconsider the relationship between risk-taking and mission fulfillment? If outside help is needed, where might the organization go to obtain assistance and what types and sources of help would be meaningful?

Risk Taking

❑ Determine if the nonprofit currently has a process in place for the formal identification of strategies, threats and opportunities. For example, some nonprofits examine mission-critical threats and opportunities during the periodic strategic planning process.

❑ Determine whether there is a stumbling block— human or otherwise—that prevents the board from thoughtfully discussing threats along with opportunities. For example, in some organizations a charismatic leader might dismiss those who, in his or her view, try to throw cold water on creative ideas. If this is true in the organization, determine how to address this individual's fear that discussion of threats will sap creativity.

❑ Make a list of fears expressed by key stakeholders. Divide the list into fears about issues that have materialized in the nonprofit's past experience or the experience of similar or neighboring organizations, and fears that seem to be remote risks. Next, identify the types of information or testimony that might prove useful in addressing the fears on the list. For example, would information on the nonprofit's safety training for volunteers and strategy for responding to volunteer injury lessen fears about the risk of volunteer injury? If not, what steps or strategies might be effective to reduce fear to an appropriate level (e.g. re-working assignments or sending volunteers on assignments in pairs rather than alone)?

❑ Assign responsibility for compiling a list of all accidents, incidents (including "near misses") and losses occurring at your nonprofit during the past five years. In a large nonprofit this project might be undertaken by the existing risk management committee. In a smaller organization, the task might be suited to an ad-hoc committee of the board or a staff team. The list should include a short description of the loss, an indication of the cause of loss (such as lack of proper training, faulty equipment), a description of post-loss changes in procedures or operations, and an indication of whether it is possible for the loss to recur. Identify the policy, training or supervisory changes that have taken place since the incident or loss to prevent its recurrence. If no changes have been made, identify a team of suitable personnel that can serve on a loss prevention task force. Consider employees, volunteers and outside advisors as possible participants in this process. Schedule a meeting to review the "loss runs" or summary of incidents and losses. Charge the team with identifying a minimum of four strategies for preventing the recurrence of each loss, assigning a price tag to each strategy, and ranking the strategies in terms of predicted effectiveness in preventing recurrence. Implement the recommendations of the loss prevention task force.

Board Communication and Leadership

❑   Review the format in which risk management information is presented to the board. Review the questions about risk and risk taking posed by the board at recent meetings. Determine if changes in the scope or format of information provided to the board are necessary to position the board as a partner in the nonprofit's risk management program.

❑   Consider whether there is a board champion for risk management. Many organizations report that when a board member delivers a presentation on a substantive topic, the board is more likely to be engaged. Would it be appropriate for the board champion to present risk management information?

❑   Reflect on recent presentations on risk management topics. Were there any signs that certain board members did not fully understand the information presented? Sometimes the board member who does not fully understand the information being presented is also reluctant to speak up. Identify ways to help the board as a whole, or individual members, better understand the presentation of risk management related information.

❏ Identify areas within your nonprofit that have not been addressed by your risk management program. For example, you may feel that the issue of screening volunteers has been adequately addressed, but not the issue of online fundraising. Think broadly about your day-to-day operations and key programs and services. Identify staff members (by functional area) in your nonprofit who have not had an opportunity to participate in risk management activities.

Resources on Strategic Risk Management

We urge readers to consult the organizations and texts listed below for additional insights on the subject of strategic risk management.

Nonprofit Risk Management Center—The Center provides free technical assistance to nonprofits on a wide range of risk management topics. This service is accessible at **www.nonprofitrisk.org** or by telephone: (202) 785-3891.

Risk and Insurance Management Society—A professional society for risk managers in the United States and Canada, offering many general resources. **www.rims.org**

Risk Management Reports—RMR is a monthly commentary on strategic risk management, written and edited by H. Felix Kloman. The publication is based on the editor's 30 years of experience as a risk management consultant, lecturer and author. **www.riskreports.com**

Risk Management Resource Center—This Web site merges the online resources of the Nonprofit Risk Management Center, the Public Risk Management Association and the Public Entity Risk Institute. **www.eriskcenter.org**

Chapter 3
Fiscal Integrity

M any nonprofits struggle every day with financial management issues. From raising enough funds to support operations, to properly recording and tracking grants and contracts, to implementing affordable financial management systems, a nonprofit's financial operations require constant care and feeding. Yet finance is one of several "administrative" functions that do not produce revenue for the organization or involve direct service delivery to clients. In recent years the call for fiscal integrity, financial accountability, and "transparency" in financial operations has increased the urgency of getting one's financial house in order. The insistence on greater financial accountability and transparency has been described as the expectation that nonprofits operate with a "glass wallet." Some financial advisors have recommended that key provisions of the Sarbanes-Oxley Act of 2002 be regarded as "best practices," despite the fact that most SOX provisions apply to publicly-traded companies only. Nonprofits operate along a vast continuum—from those that struggle to complete the Form 990 on time to those that have sophisticated financial management systems in place yet seek to generate even more effective financial reports and tools for management decision making or to improve investment strategies.

Along with employment practices, risk management, leadership sustainability and fundraising, financial management is an important concern for the nonprofit board.

While it is rare in a mature nonprofit for a board member to perform day-to-day bookkeeping or financial management duties (such as making journal entries or signing checks), board members exercise overall responsibility for the fiscal affairs of the nonprofit they serve. To discharge this responsibility board members must:

❑ Have a keen interest in the fiscal affairs of the nonprofit, including its overall, current financial position, the reliability of the reports the board receives, and the effectiveness of the nonprofit's management of incoming and outgoing funds.

❑ Require regular, timely and complete financial reports.

❑ Be in position to ask critical questions about the financial reports the board receives, including budgets, periodic financial statements, the annual Form 990 and annual, sometimes audited financial statements.

A board that fails on any of the above issues is incapable of meeting its legal duty of care. In many cases the board roster will include several people who are comfortable reviewing nonprofit financial statements. These individuals may volunteer to serve on the finance committee. Other board members may defer to these individuals and refrain from getting involved in the nonprofit's fiscal affairs. While a talented finance committee is a valuable asset, the remaining board members can never abdicate their responsibility for the fiscal affairs of the nonprofit. Any evidence that one or more board members do not understand the financial presentations should be addressed with prompt training and assistance.

What Does a Nonprofit With Fiscal Integrity Look Like?

❑ The finance committee and board receive regular financial statements that are largely error-free, easy-to-understand, and presented with sufficient information to allow careful scrutiny of the nonprofit's financial position.

❑ The finance committee and board receive a draft annual budget well in advance of the start of the fiscal year, allowing sufficient time for careful deliberation on the nonprofit's fund-raising and spending plans.

❑ The budget of the organization is adopted prior to the beginning of the fiscal year.

❑ During finance committee and budget presentations members of the board ask questions, make comments and engage in discussion that provides evidence of the board's understanding of and interest in the financial presentation and fiscal health of the nonprofit.

What Does a Nonprofit That Lacks Fiscal Integrity Look Like?

❑ The board and finance committee receive error-laden financial reports on an irregular basis. The reports contain little or no narrative information to support careful review.

❑ The staff of the organization reacts negatively to questions about financial matters, including expenditures or proposed revenue targets.

❑ Finance committee reports or presentations are generally adopted with few or no questions from other board members, who believe that it is their responsibility to defer to the committee on financial matters.

❑ The nonprofit's annual audit and tax filings are consistently behind schedule.

❑ The management letter that accompanies the annual audit includes the same follow-up items year after year.

The Board's Fiscal Integrity "To Do" List

This section offers a list of possible steps that a nonprofit board might pursue in order to address weaknesses in the nonprofit's existing financial management systems and approach. Whether the items below are suitable as board action items or items that should be handled by professional staff members depends on the history, culture, size and maturity of the organization. In addition to selecting an action step, it is vital to identify a target date for completion and the lead board or staff member for the task. Review the list and check those that are suitable to your nonprofit.

Financial Reporting

❏ Ensure that the board or finance committee receive accurate financial statements on time each month (or less frequently, such as quarterly, for very small nonprofits). Financial reports should be included in materials distributed prior to in-person or telephone meetings of the board or finance committee, allowing participants to review statements in advance and bring any questions to the meeting.

❏ Feature a discussion of financial statements as a standing agenda item at board meetings. The organization should also work towards this discussion being led by the elected board treasurer, versus a staff member. When the treasurer has reviewed the statements in advance of a meeting and is prepared to talk about them and answer any questions during the meeting, it sets a great example of fiduciary responsibility.

❏ Financial information should be made more accessible to board members by creating a simple financial statement cover sheet that summarizes key points. Simple graphs or charts can be helpful to visualize activity. For instance, a pie chart showing the expenses of key programs and activities for the period might help the board understand the organization better.

❏ Schedule a board training session on reading and understanding nonprofit financial statements. Many board members are reluctant to ask questions in a meeting for fear they will appear deficient. A good training session of even a couple of hours by a nonprofit consultant or CPA could give board members the vocabulary and confidence they need to be more engaged.

❏ If an independent audit is not currently undertaken, determine whether one is needed or prudent. Have any of the nonprofit's key stakeholders requested that an annual audit be conducted?

❏ Review the nonprofit's current and prospective funder guidelines to determine whether an annual audit is required as a condition of receiving funds. For instance, the federal government requires an audit of organizations expending more than $500,000 in federal funds within a year; some states require audits of all nonprofits, and some foundations also require them.

❏ Consider whether your organization is growing financially—both in terms of total dollars and complexity. Many organizations growing from start-up status to an established entity with a paid accounting function, a defined program or programs, and support from a variety of donors will benefit from an annual audit—even if it is not required by a funder or state regulator. The audit is an opportunity to learn and improve on accounting standards and practices.

❏ Engage the board of directors in the decision to purchase an audit. Remember that the board of directors is the "client" in an audit relationship with a CPA or firm. If the board decides (or the organization is required) to move forward to engage the services of an independent audit firm to conduct a financial statement audit, it should also establish a separate audit committee.

❑ Add the completion of an independent annual audit to the budget and work plan for the organization.

❑ Make certain that the draft and final reports prepared by the audit firm are presented to the full board of directors for review and acceptance (following initial review by the audit committee).

❑ Ask nonprofit colleagues whom they use for their annual audits. Finding an auditor with a current nonprofit practice is important because nonprofit accounting standards change periodically. Once there is a group of potential candidates, draft a Request for Proposals (RFP). The RFP tells potential auditors something about the organization and its finances, what services are needed on what timeline, etc. The RFP is what the auditors respond to in offering the board a proposal for the scope and price of the work.

❑ If an audit is already conducted, consider the following steps to increase the effectiveness of the audit. Select the action steps the organization has not already taken but would like to take in the months ahead.

■ Obtain a minimum of three bids for the audit no less than every five years.

■ Schedule an opportunity for the audit firm representative to meet with the board *without the executive director or other staff present.*

■ Establish an audit committee of the board of directors to coordinate the auditor selection process and presentation to the board. Keep in mind that paid employees of the nonprofit should not serve on the audit committee, nor should the nonprofit's volunteer Treasurer (or Finance Committee Chair). The committee should be charged with responsibility for overseeing the selection of the independent auditor and the process itself.

☐ Establish a charter (see sample below) for the audit committee that clearly delineates its responsibilities. Document the contrasting responsibilities of the audit and finance committees.

SAMPLE

Audit Committee Charter

The Board of Directors of the [Name of Nonprofit] hereby establishes an Audit Committee in accordance with the guidelines described below.

The Audit Committee shall meet at least twice annually, but more often if desired or necessary, in order to discharge its responsibilities. All meetings may be held by telephone conference call. Unless otherwise authorized by the Board, the Audit Committee shall have no power to act on behalf of the Board, but shall present its recommendations to the Board for action. The members of the Audit Committee shall be persons serving on the organization's board who have no existing financial, family or other personal ties to management of the organization. Staff members and the volunteer Treasurer of the organization may not serve on the Audit Committee.

Member qualifications include:

1. A clear understanding of the role of the [Name of Nonprofit] and its services.
2. Financial literacy/expertise (at a minimum, the ability to read and understand financial statements).
3. Courage to ask probing questions and to follow up for answers.
4. Ability to see the big picture.
5. A commitment to safeguard the organization and its assets.
6. A commitment to the staff (employees and volunteers) of the organization.
7. A commitment that the organization will report fairly, accurately, and regularly on its activities and condition.
8. Willingness to do the right thing, not just do things right.

The Audit Committee's responsibilities shall include:

1. Selecting the audit firm to conduct an independent audit of the organization's financial statements.
2. Reviewing and approving the audit scope and fees.
3. Reviewing and approving any proposed involvement of the audit firm in activities other than the annual audit.
4. Ensuring a direct line of communications with the organization's auditor.
5. Providing oversight of management's performance with respect to required and recommended financial responsibilities and disclosure.
6. Consider and review, with management and the auditors, the adequacy of the organization's risk management methodology and internal controls, including computerized information system controls and security.

continued on next page

Audit Committee Charter
continued

7. Providing oversight of the organization's conflict of interest policy and keeping the board apprised of any changes required in the policy or its implementation.
8. Reviewing the adequacy of financial reports provided by the board and making recommendations for their improvement.
9. Reviewing and addressing the management letter and auditor's comments.
10. Review any serious difficulties or disputes with management encountered during the course of the audits.
11. Review other matters related to the conduct of the audits that are to be communicated to the Committee under generally accepted auditing standards.
12. Review published documents containing the organization's financial statements and consider whether the information contained in these documents is consistent with the information contained in the financial statements.
13. Cause to be made an investigation into any matter brought to its attention within the scope of its duties, with the power to retain outside counsel for this purpose if, in its judgement, that is appropriate. The Committee will promptly report any such actions to the Executive Committee.
14. Make recommendations to the board based on the committee's review activities.

Members of the Audit Committee shall be appointed by the President and serve for two-years.

Form 990

The Form 990 is a public document and an important nonprofit accountability tool widely available on the Internet to your funders, the media, and others; ensuring that the form is completed fully, accurately and on-time is the responsibility of management and the board. Because nonprofit donors and stakeholders increasingly read the Form 990, consider the action steps listed below to improve the Form 990 and ensure the nonprofit's compliance with disclosure requirements. Check the action steps the organization has not already taken but would like to take in the months ahead.

- ❏ Distribute the draft Form 990 to the board and ask board members to review the document prior to its filing. Does the description of the program accomplishments tell the organization's *current* story? Are board members listed accurately? Is personal information about the board properly excluded (consider using the nonprofit's mailing address rather than a home address for each board member)?

- ❏ Make certain that the Form 990 is signed by the nonprofit's chief executive officer (typically the executive director or board president).

- ❏ Post the nonprofit's Form 990 on the organization's Web site (if you have one). This demonstrates full disclosure and eliminates the need to provide copies in response to requests from the public. Alternatively, inform Web site visitors how they can access your current and past Form 990s at www.guidestar.org.

- ❏ Assign someone in the nonprofit responsibility for maintaining copies of Form 990s from the last three years to be sent or given to any person who requests them, if they are not readily available on the nonprofit's Web site. Remember not to include the list of donors (Schedule B)—the only part of the Form 990 that is *not* required to be disclosed to the public.

- ❏ Ask the nonprofit's finance manager or board treasurer to visit the GuideStar Web site at www.guidestar.org. Check to see if the nonprofit's Form 990s have been posted there. Learn how to edit the various features of the organizational record so that site users find complete and accurate information about your nonprofit.

Inclusive Annual Budgeting Process

An inclusive annual budgeting process is essential to good organizational planning and results in a monitoring tool available to the board throughout the year. As the organization grows and changes, there may be ways that it can improve the annual budgeting process. Check the action steps your nonprofit has not already taken but would like to take in the months ahead.

❑ Consider whether the nonprofit's size and scope warrants the inclusion of program or department managers in the development of their own budgets. The people who run activities are the most familiar with program needs for the coming year. Involving them also means the organization can hold them accountable for monitoring their budgets throughout the year.

❑ Discuss with staff the process of starting the annual budgeting process three months before the target date for adopting the budget. Doing so will allow time to obtain meaningful input from staff and the board prior to the board meeting at which the final budget is approved.

❑ Explore ways to better forecast income. It is easy to overestimate income during the budget process, which can leave the organization scrambling during the year when reality hits. Consider whether it is practical to "discount" funding source totals that are included in your budget based on the likelihood that the nonprofit will receive them. For instance, a verbally guaranteed renewal of a foundation grant might go into the budget at 100 percent of the amount requested, but a first-time application to a government agency in a competitive process might go in at 50 percent.

❑ Deepen the board's understanding of the relationship between the organization's core programs and major funding sources. Require "program by source" budgets that anticipate how much each of the programs will draw from general unrestricted support.

Tracking Income and Expense

Tracking income and expense in the areas of program(s), administration, and fundraising is in line with Generally Accepted Accounting Principles (GAAP). Expense information must be reported this way on nonprofit audits and on your annual Form 990. This accounting approach also best reflects the way nonprofits talk about their programs and accomplishments, so functional tracking makes for useful management and board reports.

Here are some activities to consider if the organization wants to begin tracking its financial activity by function:

❑ Make sure that the board is clear on the definition of core functions (program, administration, fundraising and membership development, if applicable). Consult a nonprofit finance book or CPA/consultant for guidance.

❑ Engage key board members in defining your nonprofit's core program(s). For instance, a nonprofit homeless shelter might have three core programs: overnight shelter, meal services, and adult literacy. In this case, they would have five functions: the three program areas, plus administration and fundraising.

❑ Distinguish between the organization's functions and its funding sources. Many nonprofits confuse the two, treating each new funding source as if it were a new program. In fact, the vast majority of nonprofits have only a handful of core programs though they may have more than a dozen primary funding sources.

❑ Consider whether the nonprofit's current chart of accounts—the coding system for tracking financial activity at your organization—enables the creation of meaningful financial reports. Consider updating the chart of accounts if it does not capture income and expense information by function. For instance, many groups will find that financial data is currently tracked by source but not by function.

Managing Restricted Contributions

Managing restricted contributions is one of the trickiest parts of nonprofit financial management. Having a consistently applied approach to tracking these funds is an essential element of accountability. Here are some things to consider for improving on the system the nonprofit has in place:

❑ Budget for temporarily restricted contributions separately. During the annual budgeting process, plan for the periods during the coming year in which the organization will acquire and be able to "release" restricted funds.

❑ Confirm that the organization's system of tracking restricted support (including government contracts) is not impeding its ability to capture quality information by core function. In other words, is the board getting the financial information it needs, or is it only the nonprofit's funding sources that are satisfied? What changes in the tracking system would better support financial analysis and decision-making by the board?

❑ Determine what help the board of directors requires to better understand the organization's use of restricted funds. Does the board need training in this area? Do the financial statements provided to the board reflect the organization's current balance of restricted funds?

Recording Staff Time

For most nonprofits, staff salary expense is the largest part of the operating budget, so recording how staff time is used among the nonprofit's various activities is a crucial part of understanding full program costs, as well as producing accurate reports for funding sources. Here are some issues the Finance Committee might consider discussing with staff in order to improve the organization's time-tracking system:

❑ Are procedures in place to make sure that both the staff person and his or her supervisor sign monthly timesheets before they are filed?

❑ For those who must comply with government funding regulations, confirm that the timesheets reflect an "after-the-fact" determination of how each staff person actually spent his or her time. This means that employee time spent on each activity cannot be pre-set based on contract or grant budgets. This is also a best practice for nongovernment-funded nonprofits because it gives the most accurate picture of actual program costs.

❑ Does the nonprofit use an employee timesheet form that provides space for the employee to document the total hours worked each day by program or activity? The activity choices should correspond to the core activities in the nonprofit's accounting system.

❑ Are employees required to turn in a signed timesheet at the end of each month or with each payroll period? *Note*: although it is a good idea to require completed timesheets and hold staff accountable, legal responsibility for tracking time remains with the employer. An employee can be disciplined for failing to comply with this requirement, but that discipline should never include docking pay.

❑ Does the nonprofit require that supervisors review their employees' timesheets for accuracy and sign them?

❑ Are steps taken to ensure that employee timesheets reflect *actual* use of time rather than pre-determined or budgeted use of time?

❑ Does the nonprofit use timesheet information to accurately spread salary and related benefits costs among the organization's core activities in the accounting system?

Internal Controls

Internal controls are at the foundation of sound financial management and protection of the organization's assets. The first step with respect to the board's role is to ensure that new board members understand their roles and responsibilities in fiscal oversight—they are part of internal controls, too.

If documented internal controls are not in place at the nonprofit, determine how the board, finance committee and staff might work collaboratively on the following priority activities:

- ❑ Investigate what constitutes good internal controls and determine which categories of control are not yet in place at the nonprofit.

- ❑ Consider how the nonprofit can segregate key finance duties so that no one person is in charge of a process from start to finish. For instance, a bookkeeper may print checks but the executive director signs them. Or, a receptionist can open solicitation returns, but a bookkeeper prepares the bank deposit. Begin this effort by identifying how incoming and outgoing funds and paperwork move through the organization. Which positions are currently involved in handling or processing cash, checks, pledges, invoices, deposit paperwork and receipts?

- ❑ Consider requiring two signatures on all checks or at least checks over a certain dollar amount depending on the size of the organization.

- ❑ Develop a manual for the finance and administration policies and procedures of the nonprofit. This does not have to be fancy or expensive, but it should cover the major tasks and who is responsible for them. As the organization grows, update the manual accordingly. If a manual or policy document currently exists, review it to determine its relevancy to current operations. Consider what changes are required to bring the manual up to date.

- ❑ Involve the board of directors. The board's approval of the annual budget and monitoring of budgeted financial statements is a part of quality internal control. The board should also authorize significant expenditures or agreements such as major grant proposals, leases, and loans.

Accrual Basis of Accounting

The accrual basis of accounting—where income is recorded when earned and expenses are recorded when incurred—is consistent with *Generally Accepted Accounting Principles* (GAAP) because in most cases it is more accurate than cash basis accounting.

In cash basis accounting, income is only recorded when deposited, and expenses are only recorded when paid. Except in the very smallest of operations, reports produced out of a cash basis system *will not tell the whole financial story for the period.* For instance, there may be a stack of unpaid bills on the bookkeeper's desk that do not show up on the financial statements, thus leaving the false impression of a surplus.

Here are some activities to consider to determine if the nonprofit would benefit from moving from a cash to accrual basis of accounting, and if so, how to get started. Since generally speaking only small nonprofits use a cash basis accounting system, this list is most relevant to small nonprofits—many of whom rely heavily on board members or other volunteers for financial management help. Check applicable items that you want to add to your nonprofit's "To Do List" for fiscal integrity:

❑ Determine if the organization typically ends the month with unpaid bills or income that has been earned but not yet deposited. If it does, then there would be a meaningful difference in the organization's financial statements if switched to accrual. If the organization receives and deposits all money and receives and pays all bills within each month then there will not be a meaningful difference between cash- and accrual-based reporting.

❑ Determine if the person currently keeping the books has the bookkeeping skills to manage an accrual-based system. Does he or she need training on the concepts and/or on how to use the accounting software differently?

❑ Involve the board treasurer in the decision to switch to accrual. How will the change affect the work of the treasurer? What resources can he or she bring to the process?

❑ Choose a time for the organization's switch to an accrual-based accounting system, such as the beginning of the next fiscal year.

❑ Prepare the board and staff for new elements of the financial statements, namely accounts receivable and accounts payable. Does either group require training on these concepts? Where might the nonprofit obtain help explaining the new concepts?

Planning for Surpluses

Intentionally planning for surpluses is the best way to ensure that the organization will have reserves, without which a nonprofit is at risk of financial instability or insolvency and also limited in its ability to respond quickly to new opportunities or community needs.

Here are some activities to consider if the nonprofit already budgets to generate surpluses:

❑ The finance committee of the board generally takes the lead in drafting investment policies for the organization. How will the organization invest its surplus cash? What level of risk is it willing to take on? Are there investments that don't align with the organization's mission?

❑ The board of directors can decide to formally set aside an amount of money as a board reserve. The board can determine the rules for accessing these funds and/or adding to them. Note: Board reserves are not technically "restricted," so they will appear as unrestricted net assets on the organization's balance sheet.

Here are some activities to consider if the organization is not currently planning for surpluses:

❏ Analyze your current programs. Determine which are generating a surplus and which are not. Convene a board/staff committee to review the findings and recommend strategies for increasing profitability where possible. (Note: This analysis requires that the organization is tracking income and expense by program.)

❏ Engage the board of directors in establishing a target surplus. The board might determine, for instance, that it wants the organization to work towards having the equivalent of three months' operating expense in reserves. The board can set a timeline for accomplishing this.

❏ Review the organization's overall fund-raising strategy. Are there ways that the organization can increase its unrestricted contributions, which are the primary source of reserves for a nonprofit? Set a target percentage for increasing these contributions.

❏ Consider whether the organization has funding sources with which it can renegotiate. There may, for instance, be a government funder that has been paying the same amount for a service for three years, when in fact the nonprofit's costs have gone up each of these three years. Analyze the deficits, if any, associated with the nonprofit's key activities and use that information to make a case for increased funding from government agencies, foundations and others.

Acknowledgment: This chapter is based on the *Fiscal Integrity Module* in Pillars of Accountability, developed by Jeanne Peters of CompassPoint Nonprofit Services (www.compasspoint.org).

Resources on Fiscal Integrity

The Nonprofit Risk Management Center urges readers to consult the organizations and Web sites listed on the next page for additional insights on the subject of fiscal integrity.

Alliance for Nonprofit Management—The Alliance has published a number of Frequently Asked Questions on the subject of financial management. **www.allianceonline.org**

Clearinghouse for Volunteer Accounting Services—This organization publishes a state by state listing of accountants that provide pro bono help to nonprofits. **www.cvas-usa.org**

BoardSource—Formerly the National Center for Nonprofit Boards, BoardSource is a valuable resource for practical information, tools and best practices, training, and leadership development for board members of nonprofit organizations worldwide. The organization's Web site includes Board Briefs, Q&A, articles and publications on many nonprofit financial issues. **www.BoardSource.org**

CompassPoint—CompassPoint Nonprofit Services is a nonprofit training, consulting and research organization with offices in San Francisco and Silicon Valley. Through a broad range of services, the organization provides nonprofits with the management tools, concepts and strategies necessary to shape change in their communities. **www.compasspoint.org**

American Institute of Certified Public Accountants—The AICPA Web site includes a *Summary of the Provisions of the Sarbanes-Oxley Act of 2002, Frequently-Asked Sarbanes-Oxley Questions and Answers*, and the *Full Text of the Sarbanes-Oxley Act of 2002*. The organization hosts an annual National Not-for-Profit Industry Conference attended by hundreds of nonprofit CFOs. **www.aicpa.org**

National Center on Nonprofit Enterprise—NCNE helps managers and leaders of nonprofit organizations make wise economic decisions in order to ensure that their organizations best serve their members, clients, donors and the general public by pursuing their social missions efficiently and effectively. **www.nationalcne.org**

Chapter 4
Leadership Sustainability

I t is almost impossible to overestimate the importance of the executive director's leadership role in a nonprofit organization. Succession planning is an important tool for ensuring continuity in the leadership role. Succession plans have long been the norm in the for-profit sector, especially among publicly traded corporations. More recently, nonprofits have come to recognize the value of this tool for ensuring that there is a smooth transition between top leaders, whether those transitions are planned or happen unexpectedly.

There are three approaches to succession planning:

1. **Emergency**—A replacement approach that prepares the organization for unexpected transitions. In addition to placing an acting or interim director, it also maps out the lines of authority within the organization and identifies the communications plan that may be required.

2. **Strategic Development**—This is a longer-term approach that focuses on leadership development within the organization (usually larger organizations). Typically it is incorporated into the strategic or long-term planning efforts of the organization. This is a proactive approach that broadens leadership capacity through attention to cross-training, career development and the professional development of staff and board leaders.

3. **Departure-Defined**—As the name implies, this planning is usually driven by the planned departure of the executive, usually a retirement or other situation where the executive may make his or her departure plan public long before (six months to a year) the planned departure date.

This chapter focuses on emergency succession plans. The essential question that an emergency succession plan seeks to answer is, "What if?" What would happen if the executive director leaves through an unplanned and unexpected way (say due to health)? Who within the organization is prepared to step into that role and maintain the relationships with funders, community leaders and other stakeholders? Who in the organization would be prepared to provide appropriate oversight and direction regarding the organization's operations, programs and board liaison responsibilities?

Whether the shift in leadership is unplanned and unexpected, or predictable and planned, the transition between leaders can leave an organization in a vulnerable state. Loss of confidence in the organization's ability to fulfill commitments and respond to the needs of programs and the communities served could significantly hamper an organization's reputation and longer-term viability. The ability to recover (more quickly than not) from the shock of leader transition can be supported by having a plan and implementation strategy to have key functions and responsibilities "covered" by an alternate leader if the primary is unable to fulfill his or her responsibilities.

Ensuring leadership continuity involves:

❑ a plan,

❑ people who are prepared, and

❑ information.

The Board's Leadership Sustainability "To Do" List

This section offers a list of possible steps that a nonprofit board might pursue in order to address weaknesses in the nonprofit's existing leadership sustainability systems and approach. In addition to selecting an action step, it is vital to identify a target date for completion and the lead board or staff member for the task. Review the list and check those that are suitable to the nonprofit.

The Executive Succession Plan

By having an emergency succession plan for the executive director position the organization has taken the first step toward ensuring leadership continuity. The board should consider taking any or all of the following steps to ensure the effectiveness of its plan.

❑ Develop a statement about the need to prepare for inevitable leadership change. Emergency succession plans typically begin with such a statement.

❑ Create a statement that commits the board to assessing future leadership needs before beginning a search for a successor, if one is required. The board can help itself avoid rushing into the search.

❑ Identify candidates for interim leadership to ensure continuity and stability during a short-term absence by the executive. This will provide the board with "breathing room" to conduct a good search in the case of a permanent departure.

❑ Outline succession procedures, including:

■ the line of internal management succession to the interim executive position, if appropriate;
■ the outside organization and other contacts to identify an external interim, if needed;
■ the timeframe for making the interim appointment;
■ the timeframe for appointing a board transition committee; and
■ the role and duties of the transition committee, including:

▼ communications with stakeholders
▼ identifying a transition management consultant
▼ conducting an organizational assessment
▼ designing the search plan.

People Who Are Prepared

Having someone (or several people) prepared to assume the executive leadership role during the director's absence or to serve as an interim until a new director is named, in the case of the executive's permanent departure, is an important component of leadership sustainability. Review the following action items that might further ensure the preparation of one or more persons to lead the nonprofit:

❑ Evaluate whether the board has sufficient knowledge of the skills and abilities of current staff so that it is in position to identify one or more persons who could lead the organization on an interim basis. If not, what steps are required to educate the board and support the identification of possible interim leaders?

❑ Consider whether the designated individuals have all of the skills and abilities needed to address the executive's role on an interim basis. Would the individuals require backup in key areas? What are those areas and how would you address them? What steps can be taken now to prepare one or more individuals for service as an interim CEO?

❑ Determine whether the candidates for an interim executive position could readily outline the organization's strategic direction, and key strategies, as well as the top-most trends, challenges and opportunities that are on the executive's work agenda. Skills and abilities are the ticket to entry for the acting director's role, but understanding of the strategic direction, key goals and action plans and major factors shaping the organization are what will ensure real continuity. Ideal candidates for the role of interim CEO will have some ongoing understanding of the key assumptions that shape the leadership decisions.

❑ Ensure the board is well briefed on the key trends, challenges and opportunities issues facing your organization. In interim leadership situations, boards typically need to "step up" to complement the work of the interim or acting director. Moreover, during these situations, boards typically go into a mode of heightened oversight because the leadership mix has changed. Keeping the board abreast of trends and issues will help ensure that they have the perspective required to help guide the organization. Further, it will help ensure that the board and interim executive are not scrambling to develop a shared understanding about the key business assumptions that shape their respective action.

❑ Prepare staff to step up in an interim situation. If the acting director is drawn from the staff, his or her former role will have to be covered or delegated among others. A key question to ask is, what are you doing to strengthen the staff team to carry on in the event of the director's absence?

Critical Information Accessibility

Addressing information needs is an essential step toward ensuring leadership continuity. Review the action steps below and select those that will supplement your current level of preparedness.

❑ Develop a list of key constituents to be contacted in case of a crisis or emergency transition. In addition to staff and board members, consider service recipients, funders and vendors.

❑ Learn where the executive director's key business contacts are kept. In which computer? On paper? In a personal information system or card file? Make sure that the list is up to date.

❑ Determine the location of key corporate records and whether any of these records are off site. These records include the Articles of Incorporation, Form 1023, tax-exempt determination letter from the IRS and applicable state agencies, board minutes, Form 990 federal tax filings and applicable state filings, audit files, up-to-date files on your nonprofit's current insurance coverage, lease or mortgage agreement, and funded grants.

❑ Find out the location of any confidential files to which only the executive director has access. Know where the keys to those files are kept.

❑ Confirm that a list of computer passwords, including the executive director's, has been developed and stored in a secure but accessible location.

❑ Learn the frequency of computer file backups and where they are stored, including those that are kept off site.

❑ Confirm the location of any procedural manuals for the office or key programs.

❑ Review a list of who has signature authority and for what, and the procedures for adding names and signatures at all of the banks where your nonprofit transacts business.

❑ Determine whether the executive director's files are reasonably current, labeled and well organized. If not, a modicum of organization would be highly recommended.

❑ Determine what crucial institutional information, including key business records, is only kept "under the executive director's hat." Ensure that this wealth of information is shared or documented.

❑ Document any key donor or other relationships that only the executive director is aware of or relationships that only he or she maintains. Consider who else could or should help maintain those relationships so that, to the extent possible, those become "organizational" relationships, not just relationships with the executive director as an individual.

❑ Convene a meeting with the executive director, staff, and/or key board members with a theme of "what else should/could we be doing to ensure leadership continuity and operational sustainability in our organization?" Generate a list of additional action items, if any, resulting from the meeting.

Acknowledgment: This chapter was based on the Leadership Sustainability Module in Pillars of Accountability, developed by Don Tebbe with Tom Adams, both of TransitionGuides. The chapter introduction was based, in part, on work by Karen Gaskins Jones of JLH Associates, a TransitionGuides Senior Associate.

Resources on Leadership Sustainability

TransitionGuides—For additional information on Leadership Sustainability, visit **www.TranstionGuides.com**, a Web-based resource with tools and ideas to strengthen organizations during time of leadership change. The Web site contains model succession plans and other resources to guide boards and executives during times of leadership transition. You can also reach TransitionGuides at (301) 439-6635.

CompassPoint Nonprofit Services—CompassPoint is a nonprofit training, consulting and research organization whose Web site provides links to resources for executive leadership transitions and succession planning. **www.compasspoint.org**

Support Center for Nonprofit Management—The mission of the Support Center for Nonprofit Management is to strengthen the capacity of nonprofit and public interest organizations to fulfill their missions and vitalize their communities. The Support Center offers Executive Transition Consulting Services. **www.supportctr.org**

Center for Nonprofit Advancement—This Washington-DC based NCNA (National Council of Nonprofit Associations) affiliate has produced an informative template for emergency succession planning. The template is available at no charge at: **www.nonprofitadvancement.org/template.**

Chapter 5
Employment Practices

P erhaps more than other areas covered in this book, the
topic of the board's role in employment practices gets to
the heart of the never-ending debate on "what is the board's
versus the staff's role?" Are employment matters appropriately
within the realm of board responsibility? Does an enlightened
board take an interest and play a role in employment practices
or defer both leadership and decision making on employment
matters to the nonprofit's chief paid executive? To a large
extent, the line delineating the "board's responsibility" and the
"staff's responsibility" is one that shifts and meanders based on
organizational history, size, maturity, experience, perspective,
and culture.

A chart indicating which roles belong to staff and which
belong to the board would never be appropriate for all
nonprofits. In the employment arena, the hiring of a full-time
executive director or president is a critical moment for a
nonprofit. Duties previously performed by the board can now
be performed by a paid professional. As the staff grows in size,
additional duties and roles will shift to the staff side of the
ledger. However, in even the largest, multi-million dollar
nonprofit, it is never appropriate for the board to have little or
no responsibility for employment practices. When this happens
the board has failed to meet its minimum legal responsibility. It
is also failing the accountability imperative. Why? One of the
greatest risks facing any nonprofit with employed staff is loss
(financial or otherwise) stemming from an employment matter.

A complaint to the EEOC or local human relations board or a lawsuit alleging wrongful termination, disability-based discrimination or sexual harassment are examples. Reports from insurance carriers that sell nonprofit directors' and officers' (D&O) liability insurance indicate that employment matters are the subject most likely to drag a nonprofit board into court. Employment-related claims far exceed those against nonprofit boards for breach of fiduciary duty and other claims covered under typical D&O policies.

What Does a Board Providing Leadership on Employment Matters Look Like?

❏ The board is certain that the nonprofit's employment policies comply with applicable federal and state laws.

❏ The board follows the organization's procedure when reviewing the executive director's performance.

❏ The board annually reviews and updates its policies and procedures related to board service and consequences on noncompliance.

❏ The board ensures that the organization establishes and follows appropriate employment policies, knowing the organization must honor any promises created because they can be upheld by the court.

❏ The board raises concerns about special or preferential treatment with the executive director.

What Does a Board Neglecting Employment Matters Look Like?

❏ The board knows that the nonprofit organization does not follow procedures outlined in the employee handbook or manual.

❏ The board feels constrained by contracts; a verbal agreement and a handshake are enough when hiring the executive director.

☐ The board member who donates large sums to the organization is forgiven for meddling in day-to-day affairs and given special access to certain department directors.

☐ The board focuses all of its attention on fundraising and image-building, and ignores the risks of lawsuits alleging sexual harassment or unfair termination.

Nonprofit boards play a critical role in establishing appropriate employment policies and ensuring that the organization follows its policies. Generally, the process begins with the development of a summary of the nonprofit's employment policies in the form of an employee handbook or manual. In every instance, however, a nonprofit should seek expert help from a competent employment attorney before developing or changing any employment policies.

The Board's Employment Practices "To Do" List

This section offers a list of possible steps that a nonprofit board might pursue in order to address weaknesses in the board's oversight of employment practices. In most instances, a nonprofit board should avoid involvement in the day-to-day activities of personnel management, including hiring (other than the executive director), promotions, discipline (except when the board has a defined role in a grievance process), and terminations. The board's main concern is the adoption and implementation of personnel policies and practices of the nonprofit, not its daily personnel actions. A secondary concern is the adoption of policies that reduce the likelihood of an employment practices claim against the nonprofit, and practices that strengthen the nonprofit's position should it face a legal challenge.

In addition to selecting an action step, it is vital to identify a target date for completion and the lead board or staff member for the task. Review the list that follows and check those that are suitable to your nonprofit.

❑ Determine whether the nonprofit's personnel policies are clearly stated and well-organized in a document that is distributed to all staff members.

❑ Consider whether the nonprofit's vital employment policies are applied uniformly. Is there evidence to the contrary?

❑ Identify policies that may be routinely or occasionally disregarded. For each policy, determine whether changes in policy or practice are warranted.

❑ Evaluate the sufficiency of the nonprofit's efforts to communicate policies to employees in a clear and concise manner. Does the nonprofit rely on e-mail as a primary method for communicating vital policies? Are several communications strategies employed when vital information is being communicated?

❑ Consider and evaluate the strategies the organization has adopted to reduce the likelihood of employment-related claims and challenges. Are these strategies sufficient? Is there evidence that these strategies have helped the nonprofit avoid claims?

❑ Evaluate whether the nonprofit's employment policies comply with applicable federal and state laws. Has the nonprofit sought guidance and assurance on this matter from a qualified attorney? Does the nonprofit consult an employment law specialist any time the board contemplates changes to the handbook or other key policy document?

❑ Do board members feel comfortable raising any concerns about special or preferential treatment with the chief executive officer? Is each member of the board comfortable raising questions and seeking clarification whenever they have reason to believe that the organization's employment policies have not been followed?

□ Determine whether every board member understands the nonprofit's policies and practices concerning termination.

□ Is "gross misconduct"—conduct for which an employee may be subject to immediate dismissal— specified in the handbook? Is it clear in the manual that certain violations (such as bringing a weapon to work) constitute grounds for immediate dismissal?

□ Evaluate whether the board is sufficiently informed and educated on employment policies and practices to ensure that it fulfills its legal responsibilities.

□ Consider whether the nonprofit designs its screening process around the risks posed by a specific position versus using the same process for all employees and volunteers.

□ Evaluate the degree to which the nonprofit uses appropriate tools, such as a written interview guide, in order to avoid illegal conduct in hiring.

□ Determine whether the nonprofit conducts exit interviews with departing employees as part of its employment-related risk management efforts. If exit interviews are not currently used, consider how they can be conducted efficiently and in a manner that helps the nonprofit identify and resolve potential problems before they become part of litigation against the nonprofit.

□ Consider whether the nonprofit uses a written application for all employees. Explore the adoption of an application and related process if it is now absent.

□ Consider whether the nonprofit seeks the advice of an employment attorney (someone who does not sit on the board of directors) prior to terminating or laying off staff. If not, assist the executive director in locating a qualified employment lawyer who can provide "as needed" help on such matters.

□ Does the board conduct an annual assessment of the CEO? If not, what steps are required to include this assessment to the board's work plan?

❑ Does the CEO oversee a performance appraisal process that applies to all staff? If not, how can such a process be implemented?

Resources on Employment Practices

We urge readers to consult the organizations and texts listed below for additional insights on the subject of sound employment practices.

Nonprofit Risk Management Center—The Center provides free technical assistance to nonprofits on a wide range of risk management topics, including the subject of this chapter. This service is accessible by e-mail at **www.nonprofitrisk.org** or by telephone: (202) 785-3891.

> *Taking the High Road: A Guide to Effective and Legal Employment Practices for Nonprofits—2nd Edition*, published by the Nonprofit Risk Management Center and available at www.nonprofitrisk.org.

Society for Human Resource Management—SHRM is a membership association of human resource professionals that offers a vast array of training and published resources. SHRM membership is a worthwhile investment for leaders committed to staying abreast of changing employment laws, regulations and state-of-the-art employment practices. **www.shrm.org**

Workforce Management—This Web site offers articles and sample policies and procedures. **www.workforceonline.com**

U.S. Department of Labor—Search the Web site of the U.S. Department of Labor for information on the Family and Medical Leave Act, Americans with Disabilities Act, overtime pay and the Fair Labor Standards Act, and dozens of other topics related to employment practices. **www.dol.gov**

U.S. Equal Employment Opportunity Commission—The EEOC Web site lists information on Federal EEO laws, types of discrimination, and which entities are covered by EEO laws. **www.eeoc.gov**

Epilogue
Effective Governance Requires Accountability

Although much has been written about governing the nonprofit organization there is surprisingly little clarity or consensus about what governing behaviors, activities or styles are effective in helping a nonprofit achieve its mission. The truth is that no single approach to running a board of directors will work in all instances. Organizational culture, history, size, resources and the personalities of the people around the board table all come into play in determining the "ideal" ingredients for effective governance. Nonprofit boards are almost like living organisms that begin in one form and slowly evolve over time. Rather than focus on styles, models, paradigms or other oft-touted approaches to the "perfect board," the Nonprofit Risk Management Center discusses a continuum of outcomes.

What does an effectively governed nonprofit look like? Throughout, this book examines characteristics of effective governance through the lens of various disciplines, such as financial management, fundraising and employment practices. If we widen our scope we might discover that some of the following characteristics apply in an effectively governed nonprofit:

- ❑ The volunteer board and paid staff interact in an environment of mutual trust and respect.

- Board discussion and deliberations are characterized by a culture of candor—each board member feels empowered to ask tough questions and engage the board and staff in an open dialogue about the challenges facing the organization.

- The volunteer board is confident that the organization is staffed by a team of competent, caring professionals.

- Well-written, thoughtful and timely reports are provided to the board in order to support thoughtful decision making.

- Board meetings regularly include a candid discussion of strategie issues that affect the organization's mission, rather than focusing solely on hearing reports from staff and committees.

- The board engages in a periodic self-assessment of its efforts and effectiveness.

- The board reviews periodically its governing documents to ensure that it is following the rules that guide its operations.

- The board has adopted procedures concerning board limits and rotation which balance the need for new leadership (a fresh perspective) with the benefit of leadership continuity.

- The majority of the board are independent (e.g. not receiving ompensation from the organization or related by blood or marriage to anyone receiving funds from the organization).

What does a poorly governed organization look like? Taking a broad view we might see that:

- The board receives disorganized, incomplete reports that hinder, rather than enable it to make thoughtful decisions.

❑ The staff is distrustful of the board and therefore commits to providing minimal information in order to avoid interference by the board.

❑ The board meets infrequently, or ineffectively, perhaps spending much of its time on administrative concerns, providing a platform for members to espouse personal views.

❑ Members of the board feel uncomfortable raising and discussing difficult issues. The culture of the board is to avoid raising any topic that might cause discomfort on the part of staff or other board members.

❑ The board is ill-informed about the true risks and opportunities facing the organization, and thus operates in the dark or micro-manages the organization because the staff has not earned the board's trust.

❑ The board is too small in number to provide resources of time, experience and access to financial resources that the organiztion requires, or too large to effectively reach decisions on key issues.

❑ The delegation of authority to board committees or staff is unclear.

What are the risks of ineffective governance and the lack of true accountability? The risks of ineffective governance are as varied as the organizations in the nonprofit sector, but may include:

❑ Disinterest or dissatisfaction by key stakeholders, such as funders, participants, regulatory agencies, the community at large and third parties.

❑ Lack of trust or confidence by funders, contracting agencies, insurers and others.

❑ Frustration by paid staff members who look elsewhere for gainful employment.

❑ Apathy on the part of the board leading to the failure to scrutinize policies, programs and outcomes.

❑ Inability to cope effectively with unanticipated events, such as the loss of a primary funding stream or the sudden departure of a key leader (e.g., the board chair or executive director).

In the preceding pages, we have offered a series of steps to assess current practices and improve board accountability using risk management as a framework. We believe in a flexible approach that allows individual nonprofits to customize action steps and results. There is no one size that fits all. There is no universal deadline. There are as many variables as there are individual nonprofit organizations.

The Nonprofit Risk Management Center advises each individual nonprofit client to start somewhere and do what it can, when it can, but keep on keeping on. Divide and conquer. Take baby steps. Bite off no more than what you can swallow. Delegate. Use the Swiss cheese approach—keep making holes in the problem until the solution is reached. No matter which approach works for your board, start where the need is greatest to establish, shore up or polish your nonprofit board's pillars of accountability.

We urge readers of this book to check out the online version of *Pillars of Accountability*. In addition to providing an automated strategy for developing an accountability "to do" list, the online tool explores two subject areas not included in this text: cultural competence and dynamic programming. You can explore these and other cornerstones of accountability by visiting **www.nonprofitrisk.org**.

NOTES

NOTES

NOTES

NOTES

NOTES

NOTES

NOTES

NOTES